Technology Skills for Kids
— Building Your Technology Foundation: "Free From Malware" —

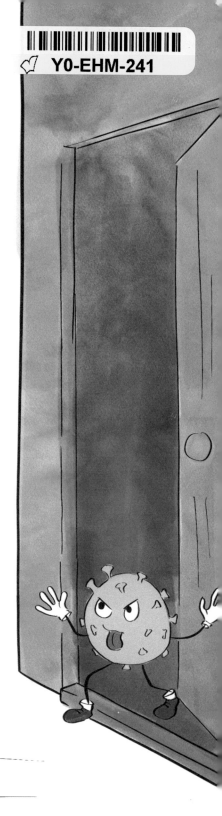

Hello and welcome!

This is **book #8** in a series of picture books created to help children make productive use of their computers and other devices while staying safe online.

Tough Cookie, Tech Wizard Mike & Tabby

Any words or phrases in **bold orange** are topics that will be explored further in this book's **supplemental materials**.

Malware, short for malicious software, is any program or file that is intentionally harmful to a computer (or mobile device).

Malware is to devices what illnesses, injuries and infections are to the human body.

"I'm here for you."

MALWARE INFECTION SYMPTOMS

POP-UP GALORE

STRANGE EMAILS

RUNS SLOWLY

WEB SEARCHES
ARE BEING REDIRECTED

CRASHES A LOT

You can often apply **The Duck Test** to malware infection.

An effective malware test is comparing how your device operates to how another person's similar device operates.

The device on the right could be infected with malware. But it could **also** be the victim of a **website scam**.

If you get any such "warning messages", power off your device and get **good help**.

Question: How do people infect their devices with malware?

Answer: Mostly by falling for scams and doing things they shouldn't.

You can infect your device with malware by visiting websites your Tabby Cat would not approve of...

YOU CAN INFECT YOUR DEVICES WITH
MALWARE BY ILLEGALLY DOWNLOADING
COPYRIGHTED MATERIALS.

Irresponsible technology use can lead to...

Here we see none other than Tech Wizard Mike infecting his new notebook with malware by taking his eye off the ball. He was not paying attention to what he was doing. Boo, Mike!

Tough Love statement: You can very easily turn any of your devices into a high-tech paperweight through irresponsible technology use.

Many people have infected their devices with malware by opening **malicious attachments**.

BE VERY CAREFUL WITH ATTACHMENTS, MY FRIEND...

Always look at an **attachment** with both eyebrows raised — even if you think it is from someone you know and trust.

Clicking or tapping one of those phony-baloney "your device is at risk" pop-up windows is an almost sure-fire way to infect your device with malware.

Unfortunately, scams, shenanigans, skullduggeries, shams, snow jobs and all the various forms of **skylarking** will never go the way of the dodo.

NOTE

Obsolete devices (due their not receiving <u>security updates</u>) are very vulnerable to malware infection.

Outsourcing the <u>administration</u> of your device is another way to get malware installed onto it and even locked out of it.

What are some common forms of malware?

Some forms of malware are scarier than others but no form of malware on your device should be acceptable. It is all dangerous.

AUTOMATED "BOTS" CRUISE THE WORLD WIDE WEB
LOOKING FOR ACCOUNTS THAT ARE EASILY
BROKEN INTO.

Adware is software that automatically displays or downloads advertising material (often unwanted) when a user is online.

A Trojan Horse Virus is a type of malware that downloads onto a computer disguised as a legitimate program.

Spyware is software that enables a user to obtain covert information about another's computer activities by transmitting data covertly from their hard drive.

Do not engage. Do not click or tap anything. Do not do anything the ransomware threat tells you to do. Power off your device and get some good help.

"Brandon" and "Edna" had downloaded and installed some shady software onto their device.

NOTE

Unfortunately scams and shenanigans will never go the way of the dodo.

Some forms of malware actually **masquerade** as software applications that promise to speed up your device and make it safer to use — and then they proceed to do just the opposite!

Such an application can be the proverbial wolf in sheep's clothing!

Five ways to help avoid infecting your devices with malware.

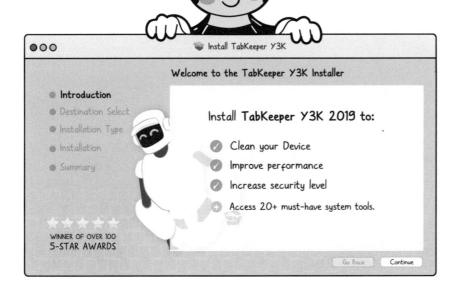

1. "Bee careful" what you download to your devices.

2. Look at all "too good to be true" offers with both eyebrows raised...

3. Do not fall for scams.

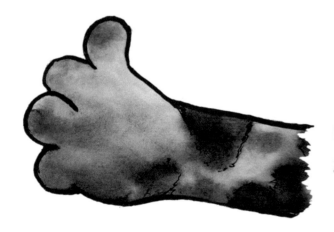

Rule of thumb: If something seems too good to be true, it most likely will be.

4. Keep your technology use squeaky clean.

Question : What is "squeaky-clean technology use"?

Answer: Pretty much the opposite of things like this.

Tech Wizard's Disco Polka

Favorites

Includes

LOVE IS BLUE
BEER BARREL POLKA
HOW HIGH THE MOON
LOVER'S CONCERTO
THE WORLD IS WAITING
WAIT TIL THE SUN SHINES
PALOMA BLANCA
CLARINET POLKA
I WANT MORE COFFEE

S. Stay in your device's Music and Movies Store(s) which will be accessible through an app on your device.

Stay in your device's **App Store** when it comes to downloading new apps to your device. If an app you need to use for school is not in your device's App Store, get some **good help**.

What about third-party virus protection software?

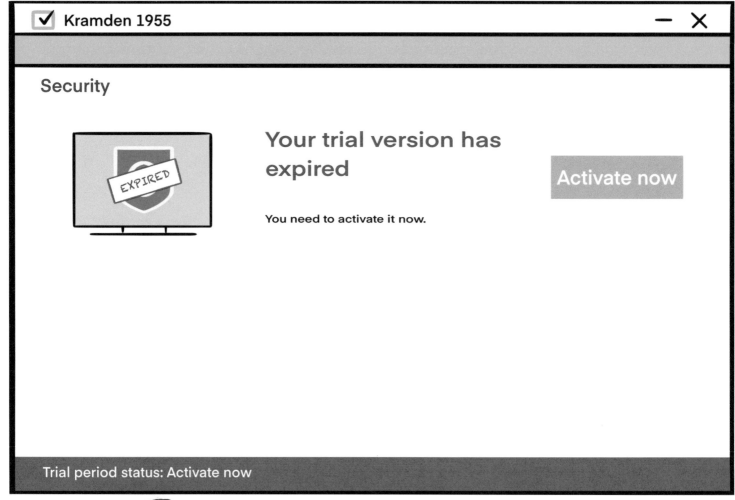

 Third-party software refers to the software that is built by a company <u>other</u> than the company that developed the system's OS.

Tech Wizard
Mike
does not
use any
third-party
virus
protection
software.

OCULUS   — X

Tasks   Settings   Performance   feedback   Account   Support

SECURITY   IDENTITY   BACKUP   TUNEUP

Subscription required
Your Computer is at Risk

RENEW NOW

 OCULUS antivirus

Subscription Status:
0 DAYS REMAINING
RENEW

Some people (especially know-it-alls) think your tech wizard friend is crazy and believes in UFOs because he does not use any third-party virus protection software.

Many devices (including Windows computers) come with free, **built-in** privacy and security protection.

What can you do if you think your device is infected with malware?

You can **factory reset** your device to rid it of malware.

(You will not have to do anything like this!)

A factory reset will restore a device to its "like new" state. This means it will erase all of your settings and content.

1. Back up your files.
2. Reset your device.
3. Practice squeaky-clean technology use henceforward.

A factory reset (however that is accomplished on your particular device) can also rid it of **bloatware**.

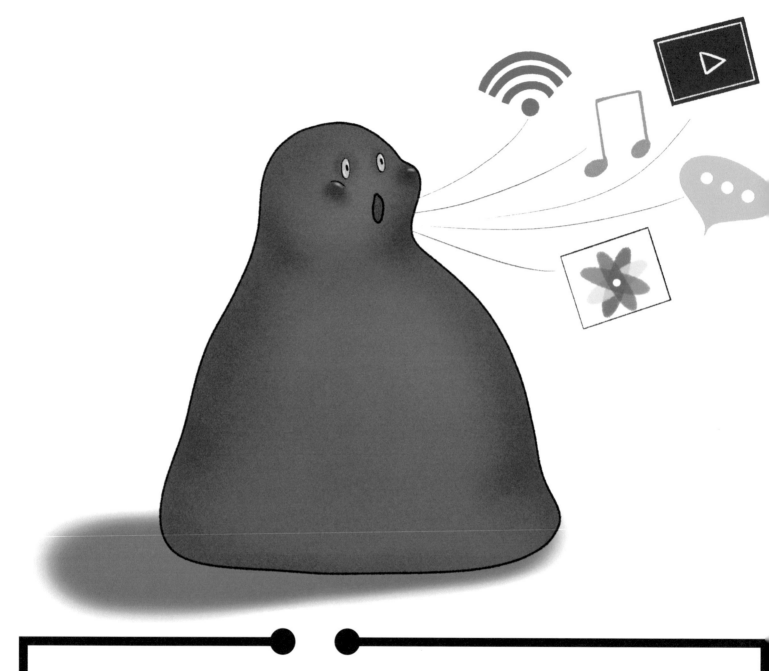

Bloatware is unnecessary software that burdens and slows down your device.

What you can do if something unexpected happens during your technology use...

1. Write down the threat or issue into your technology notebook.

2. Search the web for possible solutions.

3. Carefully follow the instructions to remove the threat.

4. If the threat persists, get some **good help**.

"No matter how pretty your theory is, if it doesn't agree with experiment, it's wrong."

True friends respect you and will
stand by you.

Work for a cause...

...not for applause.

@henryvierag

Name: _____   Date: _____

Quiz for Technology Skills for Kids - Book #8
~ MALWARE ~

Choose the right word.

malware

- malicious software
- mindful tech use

pop-up ads

AD !

- more stuff to buy!
- possible malware infection

You won!

FREE TABLET

→ CLICK HERE ←

- woo-hoo!
- scam

malware-infection cause

ERROR! ✗

- falling for scams
- using common sense

illegal downloads

- what's the harm?
- don't.

"old" devices are...

- cool!
- vulnerable

device becomes "high-tech paperweight"

- can't happen
- through Irresponsible technology use

evil email attachments

- dangerous!
- my contacts would never send one

ransomware

- better pay up!
- do not engage.

Email **techwizardmike@gmail.com** for the accompanying quiz and answer key for this book (print-ready PDFs).

Name: _____   Date: _____

ACTIVITY FOR TECHNOLOGY SKILLS FOR KIDS - BOOK #8

Sick device!

slow

redirected web searches

warning messages

crashes

Email **techwizardmike@gmail.com** for the accompanying activity and answer key for this book (print-ready PDFs).

Visit **www.technologyskillsforkids.com** for more tech skills for kids including blog posts, videos and **book #9** in this series in which we talk about file management.